Table Of Contents

Chapter 2: Setting Up for Success 1
Chapter 3: The Technology Behind AI Models 1
Chapter 4: Crafting Compelling Content 1
Chapter 5: Growing Your Audience 1
Chapter 6: Monetizing Your AI Model 1
Chapter 7: Navigating Legal and Ethical Considerations 1
Chapter 8: Scaling Your AI Model Business 1
Chapter 9: Future Trends in AI Modeling 1
Chapter 10: Real-Life Success Stories 1
Chapter 1: The Rise of AI Models 1

Chapter 1: The Rise of AI Models

Understanding AI-Generated Models

Understanding AI-Generated Models is an exciting journey into the future of digital marketing and social media. These virtual models, created using advanced AI technology, are revolutionizing how brands interact with audiences. They possess the charm, beauty, and presence of real-life influencers but operate without the constraints of human limitations. Imagine having a model who can be available 24/7, never ages, and can be customized to fit any brand's aesthetic. This is the magic of AI-generated models, and they are making waves in various industries, particularly in fashion, beauty, and lifestyle.

These AI models are not only visually stunning but also incredibly versatile. They can be programmed to embody different styles, personalities, and even moods, providing brands with a unique way to engage with their target audience. Companies can create tailored content that resonates with their followers while maintaining a consistent brand image. By leveraging AI-generated models, businesses can enhance their marketing strategies and reach new heights in brand recognition and customer loyalty. The ability to generate content at scale without sacrificing quality is a game-changer for anyone looking to make money in this digital space.

Social media platforms like Instagram are the perfect playground for these virtual models. With millions of users scrolling through their feeds daily, AI-generated models can capture attention and drive engagement like never before. They can participate in trending challenges, collaborate with other influencers, and even react to current events, all while maintaining a curated persona. This level of interaction allows brands to stay relevant and connect with their audience in real-time, ultimately leading to increased sales and profitability. The potential for virality is immense, and savvy entrepreneurs can harness this power for tremendous financial gain.

Moreover, the rise of AI-generated models presents unique opportunities for monetization. Brands can partner with these digital influencers for sponsored posts, product placements, and even entire marketing campaigns. Since AI models can be designed to fit any niche, from high fashion to everyday lifestyle, the possibilities are endless. Entrepreneurs can create their own AI models or collaborate with existing ones to establish a strong online presence. This not only opens new revenue streams but also allows for creative collaborations that can captivate audiences and drive brand loyalty.

In conclusion, understanding AI-Generated Models is crucial for anyone looking to profit from this innovative trend. By embracing this technology, businesses can position themselves at the forefront of the digital marketing landscape. The combination of creativity, technology, and strategic thinking will empower entrepreneurs to build successful ventures that resonate with audiences and generate significant income. The future of social media marketing is here, and those who seize this opportunity will undoubtedly reap the rewards of their forward-thinking approach.

The Evolution of Virtual Influencers

The rise of virtual influencers marks a revolutionary shift in the landscape of social media marketing. These computer-generated characters have begun to captivate audiences with their lifelike appearance and relatable personas. As brands increasingly seek innovative ways to connect with consumers, virtual influencers offer a unique solution that combines the best of technology and marketing. By leveraging artificial intelligence and advanced graphics, these digital models are not only visually stunning but also meticulously crafted to resonate with specific demographics, creating opportunities for businesses to engage with audiences in entirely new ways.

From the early days of simple CGI characters to the sophisticated virtual influencers we see today, this evolution has been rapid and transformative. Pioneers like Lil Miquela and Shudu Gram emerged as trailblazers, showcasing the potential of AI-generated models to generate authentic interactions and brand partnerships. Their success demonstrated that virtual influencers could command attention, spark conversations, and even build loyal followings, all while remaining entirely digital. This shift has opened the floodgates for brands to explore creative collaborations that were once unimaginable, paving the way for a new era of marketing strategies.

As virtual influencers continue to evolve, their ability to adapt to trends and consumer preferences has become a key driver of their success. Unlike traditional models, virtual influencers can be programmed to embody various styles, personalities, and narratives, allowing brands to tailor their messaging with precision. This adaptability not only ensures that virtual influencers remain relevant but also enhances their appeal as marketing tools. Brands can now craft campaigns that are not only visually appealing but also emotionally resonant, tapping into the desires and aspirations of their target audiences.

The financial implications of this evolution are staggering. Brands that embrace virtual influencers can significantly reduce costs associated with traditional marketing campaigns, including travel, logistics, and talent fees. Moreover, the ability to produce content consistently and at scale means that brands can maintain a constant presence in the digital space, engaging with followers around the clock. As a result, businesses can achieve higher returns on investment and maximize their marketing budgets, all while harnessing the power of AI-generated models to create a lasting impact.

Looking ahead, the future of virtual influencers is bright, with endless possibilities for innovation and profitability. As technology continues to advance, we can expect even more lifelike representations and interactive experiences that blur the lines between reality and virtuality. For entrepreneurs and marketers, this presents an exciting opportunity to capitalize on a growing trend and establish a foothold in the world of AI-generated models. By understanding the evolution of virtual influencers and embracing their potential, anyone can unlock new pathways to success in the dynamic realm of social media marketing.

Why AI Models Are Taking Over Social Media

AI models are revolutionizing the landscape of social media, and the reasons behind this transformation are as exciting as they are profitable. First and foremost, these virtual models possess an uncanny ability to engage audiences in ways that traditional influencers cannot. With their meticulously crafted appearances and personalities, AI models captivate followers with stunning visuals and relatable content. As they become more sophisticated, they can mimic human behavior, respond to comments, and even participate in trending challenges, drawing in massive followings. This capability not only enhances user engagement but also provides brands with a unique opportunity to connect with their target audiences on a deeper level.

The cost-effectiveness of AI models is another compelling factor driving their dominance on platforms like Instagram. Brands are constantly on the lookout for ways to reduce marketing expenses while maximizing impact. By utilizing AI-generated models, companies can eliminate the need for costly photoshoots, travel arrangements, and unpredictable influencer behavior. These virtual models are available 24/7, allowing brands to maintain a consistent online presence without the hassle of coordinating schedules or dealing with human limitations. This level of efficiency opens doors for entrepreneurs to tap into new revenue streams by partnering with AI models and offering their services to brands aiming to elevate their social media strategy.

Moreover, the versatility of AI models is a game-changer for niche marketing. Businesses can create or customize AI models to fit specific demographics, styles, or trends, allowing them to target their audience with laser precision. Whether it's a fashion-forward virtual influencer promoting the latest streetwear or a fitness-focused AI model sharing workout tips, the possibilities are endless. This adaptability empowers brands to stay relevant in an ever-evolving market, ensuring that they can consistently attract attention and drive sales. By embracing AI models, entrepreneurs can carve out their own niche and establish a foothold in the competitive world of social media marketing.

As AI technology continues to evolve, so does the potential for monetization. AI models can generate a wide array of revenue streams, from sponsored posts and brand collaborations to merchandise sales and affiliate marketing. With their ability to create content that resonates with audiences, AI models can help drive traffic to websites and increase conversion rates. This creates a win-win situation for both brands and entrepreneurs, as they can leverage the popularity of AI models to amplify their marketing efforts and boost profits. The integration of AI into social media marketing is not just a trend; it's a seismic shift that presents unprecedented opportunities for financial success.

In conclusion, the takeover of social media by AI models is not only inevitable but also incredibly lucrative. Their engaging nature, cost-effectiveness, versatility, and potential for monetization make them a powerful asset for anyone looking to profit in the digital age. As the landscape of social media continues to shift, those who embrace the rise of AI models will find themselves at the forefront of a new era in marketing. By harnessing the power of these virtual influencers, entrepreneurs can unlock new possibilities for growth and success, setting themselves apart in a crowded marketplace. The future is bright for those ready to dive into the world of AI-generated models and seize the opportunities it presents.

Chapter 2: Setting Up for Success

Identifying Your Niche

Identifying your niche is the first exhilarating step toward becoming an Insta-Millionaire with AI-generated models. In the vast and colorful world of social media, where trends change faster than the blink of an eye, honing in on a specific niche allows you to carve out your own space and attract a dedicated audience. The beauty of AI-generated models is that they can be tailored to fit any niche you can imagine, from fashion and beauty to fitness and lifestyle. Embrace the excitement of discovering what resonates with you and your potential followers, as this is where the magic begins!

To start, think about your passions and interests. What excites you? What do you enjoy sharing with others? This self-reflection is crucial because it lays the foundation for your niche. If you're a fashion enthusiast, you might consider creating AI models that showcase the latest trends or even delve into sustainable fashion. On the other hand, if you're passionate about fitness, why not develop AI models that inspire others with workout routines and healthy living tips? The key is to choose a niche that genuinely interests you, as your enthusiasm will shine through and attract followers who share your passions.

Next, it's imperative to research your chosen niche thoroughly. Dive into social media platforms, particularly Instagram, to analyze existing accounts that focus on your area of interest. What type of content are they producing? How are they engaging their audience? Identify gaps in the market or areas where you can offer something fresh and exciting. The insights you gather during this research phase will guide you in fine-tuning your niche, ensuring that you stand out in a sea of similar accounts. Remember, the goal is to create a unique identity for your AI models that captivates your audience's attention.

Once you've identified your niche and gathered insights, it's time to experiment! Create a variety of AI-generated models and content styles to see what resonates most with your audience. This is where creativity meets analytics. Track engagement rates, comments, and shares to determine which types of posts attract the most attention. Embrace the iterative process; sometimes, trial and error can lead to unexpected yet rewarding discoveries. By actively engaging with your audience, you can refine your niche further based on their feedback and preferences.

Ultimately, identifying your niche is not just about picking a topic; it's about building a community around your AI-generated models.

As you refine your niche and understand your audience's needs, your potential for monetization grows exponentially. Whether through brand partnerships, sponsored posts, or selling digital products, the opportunities are endless. So, dive in, explore, and let your passion guide you to profitability. The world of AI-generated models awaits, and your unique niche is the key to unlocking your Insta-Millionaire journey!

Creating an Engaging Profile

Creating an engaging profile is the cornerstone of attracting attention and building a following on social media, especially when leveraging AI-generated models. Your profile is the first impression potential followers and brands will have of your virtual persona. To captivate your audience, it's essential to curate a visually appealing and cohesive aesthetic that reflects your brand identity. Use high-quality images that showcase your AI model in various settings, and ensure that the colors, themes, and overall vibe resonate with the niche you are targeting. A visually stunning profile not only draws people in but also encourages them to explore your content further.

Next, your bio is crucial in conveying who your AI model is and what they represent. This is your chance to communicate your unique selling points in a concise yet engaging manner. Incorporate keywords that align with your niche to enhance discoverability. Consider adding a touch of personality or humor to make the bio memorable. Don't forget to include a call-to-action, encouraging visitors to follow your journey or check out specific content. A well-crafted bio can transform casual visitors into loyal followers eager to see what your AI model will do next.

Engagement goes beyond just aesthetics and bio; it's about interaction too. Make your profile a hub of activity by regularly posting diverse content. Use a mix of images, videos, and stories to keep things fresh and exciting. Collaborate with other creators, whether they are human or AI-generated, to expand your reach and introduce your profile to new audiences. Engage with your followers by responding to comments and messages, which not only fosters community but also enhances loyalty. Remember, an interactive profile encourages followers to stay engaged and invested in your content.

Additionally, leverage trending topics and challenges within your niche to keep your profile relevant and relatable. Stay updated on the latest trends in social media, especially those that resonate with your target demographic. By participating in popular challenges or utilizing trending hashtags, your AI model can tap into broader conversations and attract new followers who are interested in those trends. This approach not only enhances visibility but also positions your AI model as a current and engaging figure within the social media landscape.

Finally, consistency is key to maintaining an engaging profile. Develop a content calendar that outlines when and what you will post to keep a steady stream of content flowing. Consistency in posting frequency helps your followers know what to expect and when to expect it. Over time, this builds anticipation and loyalty, as followers look forward to your upcoming posts. By ensuring that your AI model's profile remains active, visually appealing, and responsive, you're setting the stage for growth and profitability in the exciting world of AI-generated models on social media.

Building a Brand Around Your AI Model

Building a brand around your AI model is an exhilarating journey that can lead to immense opportunities in the digital landscape. Your AI model is not just a digital creation; it's a persona that can captivate audiences, engage followers, and, most importantly, drive revenue. To start, focus on defining a unique identity for your AI model. Consider its style, personality, and the message it conveys. This identity will be the cornerstone of your brand and will enable you to stand out in a crowded market. The more relatable and appealing your model is, the more likely it will attract a loyal following.

Once you have established your AI model's identity, it's time to curate its content strategy. This involves creating visually stunning posts that reflect your model's unique personality and resonate with your target audience. Utilize high-quality images, engaging captions, and trending hashtags to enhance visibility. Consistency is key; maintain a regular posting schedule to keep your audience engaged. Additionally, consider leveraging features like Instagram Stories and Reels to showcase your model in dynamic ways. This approach not only builds a strong brand presence but also fosters a community around your AI model.

Engagement is crucial when building a brand. Interacting with followers through comments, direct messages, and polls can significantly enhance their connection to your AI model. Host Q&A sessions or live streams where your AI model "speaks" to the audience, providing them with a personalized experience. This interaction fosters loyalty and encourages followers to share your content with their own networks, effectively broadening your reach. Remember, the goal is to create a two-way communication channel that makes followers feel valued and connected to your brand.

Partnerships and collaborations can propel your AI model's brand to new heights. Reach out to influencers, brands, or creators who align with your model's identity and values. Collaborations can take various forms, from joint giveaways to co-created content. These partnerships not only increase your model's visibility but also lend credibility and attract new followers who are already engaged with the collaborating entities. When executed thoughtfully, these collaborations can turn your AI model into a household name.

Lastly, don't underestimate the power of analytics in brand building. Use tools to track engagement metrics, follower growth, and content performance. Understanding what resonates with your audience will allow you to refine your strategy and optimize your content. Celebrate small milestones along the way, whether it's a certain number of followers or a successful campaign. These achievements reflect the growth of your AI model's brand and provide motivation to keep pushing forward. With dedication, creativity, and a strategic approach, your AI model can become a profitable and influential brand in the world of social media.

Chapter 3: The Technology Behind AI Models

Overview of AI and Machine Learning

Artificial Intelligence (AI) and Machine Learning (ML) are revolutionizing the way we interact with technology, creating exciting opportunities for entrepreneurs and influencers alike. These powerful tools enable the generation of hyper-realistic virtual models that can capture the attention of audiences on social media platforms like Instagram. Imagine having a model that not only looks stunning but can also engage with followers, promote products, and even build a personal brand—all without the limitations of a physical presence. This is the future of marketing, and it's time to dive into how you can profit from it.

At the heart of this transformation is the ability of AI algorithms to learn from vast amounts of data. Machine learning, a subset of AI, empowers systems to improve their performance over time by analyzing patterns and making predictions. In the context of virtual models, this means that the more data these models have—such as user interactions, preferences, and trending styles—the better they become at mimicking real human behavior. The result? A captivating, interactive experience for followers that drives engagement and brand loyalty.

Creating an AI-generated model is not just about aesthetics; it's about strategy. These virtual personas can be tailored to fit specific niches, appealing to targeted demographics. Whether you're in fashion, fitness, or lifestyle, the possibilities are endless. Leveraging AI allows you to create content that resonates with your audience, engages them in meaningful ways, and ultimately converts followers into customers. This strategic approach is what sets successful entrepreneurs apart in the rapidly evolving digital landscape.

Furthermore, the economic potential of AI-generated models is enormous. Brands are increasingly turning to virtual influencers for marketing campaigns, as they offer unique benefits such as 24/7 availability, consistency in messaging, and the ability to reach global audiences without the logistical challenges of traditional models. The cost-effectiveness of maintaining a virtual model compared to a real-life counterpart opens up new avenues for monetization, whether through sponsored posts, affiliate marketing, or collaborations with brands looking to tap into the virtual influencer trend.

As we explore the exciting world of AI and machine learning, it's essential to understand the tools and platforms available to bring your virtual model to life. From advanced graphic design software to social media management tools, the resources at your fingertips are vast. Embracing this technology not only positions you as a forward-thinking entrepreneur but also allows you to harness the immense power of AI to create, market, and profit from your very own AI-generated model. The future is bright for those ready to seize this opportunity, and the time to start is now!

Tools and Software for Model Creation

The world of AI-generated models is not just a trend; it's a revolution that is transforming the way we think about digital content and social media. To dive into this exciting realm, you need the right tools and software that can help you create stunning, lifelike models that can captivate audiences on platforms like Instagram. The right tools not only enhance your creative process but also streamline your workflow, allowing you to focus on what truly matters: generating revenue through these innovative digital personas.

One of the most popular software choices for creating AI-generated models is Daz 3D. This powerful platform allows users to design customizable 3D characters with realistic features and expressions. The extensive library of assets, including clothing, hairstyles, and accessories, means that your models can be tailored to fit any niche or aesthetic. With its user-friendly interface, Daz 3D empowers both beginners and seasoned artists to bring their visions to life effortlessly, making it a must-have tool for anyone looking to profit from virtual models.

Another fantastic tool in your arsenal is Adobe Photoshop, a staple for digital artists. While it's widely known for photo editing, Photoshop's capabilities extend to creating and enhancing your AI-generated models. You can refine textures, adjust lighting, and manipulate images to achieve that perfect look that resonates with your target audience. By combining Photoshop with 3D modeling software, you can produce images that stand out in a crowded social media landscape, drawing attention and engagement to your brand.

For those looking to add a touch of interactivity to their models, Blender is an excellent option. This open-source 3D creation suite offers robust animation and rendering capabilities. You can animate your models to create eye-catching videos or GIFs that will make your social media posts pop. Blender's flexibility allows for the integration of various effects and enhancements, ensuring that your models are not just visually appealing but also dynamic and engaging. The learning curve may be steep, but the potential for creativity and innovation is limitless.

Lastly, don't overlook the power of AI-based platforms like Artbreeder or Runway ML. These tools leverage machine learning to generate and manipulate images, providing a fresh and unique perspective on model creation. Artbreeder allows you to blend images and create entirely new characters, while Runway ML offers advanced features for video and image generation. By incorporating these AI-driven tools, you can stay ahead of the competition and continuously produce fresh content that captivates and converts your audience into loyal followers and customers. Embrace these tools, and watch as your virtual models thrive on social media, opening up new avenues for profit and creativity.

Tips for Customizing Your AI Model

Customizing your AI model to stand out in the crowded landscape of social media is an exciting endeavor! The first step to personalization is to define the personality and style of your AI model. Think about the niche you want to target and the audience you wish to attract. Do you want your model to exude elegance, fun, or perhaps an edgy vibe? Creating a detailed character profile will not only help in crafting engaging content but will also resonate with your followers. The more authentic your AI model feels, the more likely it is to capture the attention of your audience and drive engagement.

Next, focus on the visual aspects of your AI model. The aesthetics of your model are crucial for making a memorable impression. Utilize advanced tools to customize facial features, hairstyles, and outfits that align with current trends. Pay attention to color schemes and backgrounds that complement your model's personality. This is where the magic happens — a visually stunning AI model can captivate followers at first glance. Utilize platforms that allow for seamless updates and changes to keep your model fresh and aligned with evolving trends and seasons.

Content is king, and this holds true for your AI model as well. Strategically plan your posts to showcase your model in a variety of settings and scenarios. Create narratives or themes that can be followed from one post to the next, giving your audience a reason to stay engaged. Don't hesitate to experiment with different types of content such as stories, reels, and collaborations. The more diverse and dynamic your content is, the more likely it is to attract a wider audience. Remember, the goal is to create a connection with your followers, so let your model's personality shine through in every post.

Engagement is another key factor in customizing your AI model. Interacting with your audience will create a sense of community and loyalty. Encourage followers to comment on your posts, participate in polls, or share their thoughts on your model's adventures. Use analytics tools to track what types of content resonate most with your audience. This data can provide invaluable insights into their preferences, allowing you to tailor your approach even further. The more you listen to your audience, the better you can customize your model to meet their desires.

Finally, don't forget to leverage the power of storytelling. Every successful brand has a compelling story behind it, and your AI model is no different. Share the journey of your model, from its conception to its daily life on social media. This narrative can be woven into your posts and can help humanize your virtual influencer. By connecting emotionally with your audience, you create a deeper bond that can lead to increased loyalty and, ultimately, profit. Remember, the more effort you put into customizing your AI model, the greater the potential for success in the dynamic world of AI-generated influencers!

Chapter 4: Crafting Compelling Content

Types of Content That Attract Followers

In the world of social media, particularly on platforms like Instagram, the content you create is the lifeblood of your engagement and follower growth. To truly attract followers, it's essential to focus on specific types of content that resonate with your audience. One of the most effective strategies is to harness the power of visually stunning imagery. High-quality photos, whether featuring AI-generated models in glamorous settings or showcasing unique fashion styles, can captivate users as they scroll through their feeds. The more eye-catching and professional your images are, the more likely they are to be shared, liked, and commented on, driving up your visibility.

Another content type that can significantly boost your follower count is storytelling through captions. Pairing your striking visuals with engaging narratives allows you to connect with your audience on a deeper level. Share the journey of your AI models, their inspirations, and the creative process behind the scenes. Personal anecdotes or fun facts about your models can create a sense of familiarity and relatability that followers crave. When you evoke emotions through storytelling, you not only attract followers but also build a loyal community that feels invested in your brand.

Interactive content is also a game-changer. Polls, quizzes, and challenges can encourage your audience to engage actively with your posts. Consider hosting a weekly challenge featuring your AI models where followers can participate by sharing their interpretations or styling tips. This not only generates excitement but also encourages user-generated content, which is a powerful tool for attracting new followers. When users see their peers participating and having fun, they are more likely to join in, expanding your reach and fostering a vibrant online community.

Video content deserves special mention as well. Short clips showcasing your AI models in action, whether it's a fashion walk, a makeup tutorial, or a lifestyle vignette, can be incredibly engaging. Platforms like Instagram Reels and Stories thrive on dynamic video content, allowing you to showcase your creativity and the versatility of your AI models. The potential for viral growth is enormous when you produce content that is not only entertaining but also informative and visually appealing. Embrace trends in video production, and don't hesitate to experiment with different formats to see what resonates best with your audience.

Lastly, collaborations with other influencers or brands can propel your follower growth to new heights. Partnering with established names in the industry can introduce your content to a broader audience. Joint giveaways, photo shoots, or even co-created content can create buzz and attract followers who are eager to discover fresh accounts. These partnerships can also lend credibility to your brand, making it easier for new audiences to trust your AI-generated models and engage with your content. By diversifying your content strategy and embracing these various types of content, you can effectively attract followers and set the stage for monetization in the exciting world of AI-generated models.

The Art of Storytelling with AI Models

The art of storytelling with AI models is revolutionizing the way brands connect with their audiences on social media platforms like Instagram. Imagine scrolling through your feed and encountering stunning visuals of models that not only capture attention but also tell a compelling story. These AI-generated models can be crafted to embody diverse personalities, lifestyles, and aspirations, creating narratives that resonate deeply with followers. By leveraging the power of storytelling through these digital personas, businesses can build stronger connections and drive engagement in ways that traditional models simply cannot.

One of the most exciting aspects of using AI models is their ability to adapt and evolve through user interactions. Each post, comment, and share provides valuable data that can be analyzed to refine their narratives further. This dynamic storytelling approach allows brands to create personalized experiences that cater to specific audience segments. By understanding what resonates with their followers, businesses can tailor their content strategies to enhance engagement and loyalty, ultimately leading to increased profitability.

Moreover, the storytelling potential of AI models extends beyond mere visuals. These digital influencers can share their journeys, struggles, and triumphs through authentic and relatable narratives. By crafting a storyline that aligns with the values and dreams of their target audience, brands can foster emotional connections that drive consumer behavior. This emotional engagement is crucial in today's marketplace, where consumers are increasingly looking for authenticity and relatability in the brands they support.

Incorporating AI-generated models into a brand's marketing strategy also opens up endless creative possibilities. From fashion and beauty to travel and lifestyle, these models can be placed in various contexts that highlight products and services in unique ways. The ability to tell diverse stories allows brands to reach wider audiences and explore different niches. Whether it's showcasing a new clothing line or promoting a travel destination, the storytelling capabilities of AI models can create immersive experiences that captivate and inspire.

To maximize the impact of storytelling with AI models, brands should embrace collaboration with content creators and influencers. By combining the authenticity of real influencers with the creativity of AI-generated models, brands can create powerful campaigns that leverage the strengths of both worlds. This synergy not only amplifies reach but also enriches the storytelling experience, allowing brands to capture the imagination of their audience while driving sales. In the ever-evolving landscape of social media, mastering the art of storytelling with AI models is not just a trend; it's a game-changing strategy that can lead to significant profits for savvy entrepreneurs.

Scheduling and Consistency for Maximum Impact

In the fast-paced world of social media, consistency is key to capturing attention and retaining followers. For those leveraging AI-generated models on platforms like Instagram, scheduling posts strategically can amplify your impact and drive engagement to new heights. By establishing a regular posting routine, you not only keep your audience engaged but also create anticipation around your content. Imagine your followers eagerly awaiting each new post, excited to see what your virtual models have to offer! This consistency builds trust and familiarity, which are essential for converting followers into loyal customers.

To maximize the impact of your AI-generated models, it's crucial to identify the best times to post. Analyzing your audience's activity patterns can reveal when they are most active and engaged. Utilize analytics tools to track peak engagement times, and schedule your posts accordingly. This data-driven approach ensures that your content reaches the widest audience possible. Remember, the goal is to meet your audience where they are, and strategic timing can make all the difference in driving traffic to your profile and ultimately increasing your revenue.

Engagement doesn't stop at posting; it extends to your interactions with followers. Consistency in responding to comments and messages fosters a sense of community around your AI models. By actively engaging with your audience, you not only increase the likelihood of repeat interactions but also create a personal connection that can enhance your brand's appeal. That human touch, combined with the allure of your virtual models, can lead to a loyal following that is eager to support your monetization efforts.

Incorporating a content calendar can further enhance your scheduling strategy. Planning your posts in advance allows you to curate a cohesive aesthetic and narrative around your AI-generated models. This foresight enables you to align your content with seasonal trends, holidays, or events that resonate with your audience. By being proactive in your scheduling, you can ensure that your posts are not only timely but also relevant, keeping your followers engaged and interested in your offerings.

Ultimately, the synergy of scheduling and consistency can propel your journey to becoming an Insta-millionaire. By maintaining a disciplined approach to posting and engaging with your audience, you create an ecosystem where your AI-generated models can thrive. The combination of strategic timing, community engagement, and thoughtful content curation paves the way for increased visibility and profitability. Embrace these principles, and watch as your social media presence transforms into a lucrative venture that capitalizes on the power of AI models.

Chapter 5: Growing Your Audience

Strategies for Gaining Followers

Building a robust follower base is essential for anyone looking to profit from AI-generated models on platforms like Instagram. One of the most effective strategies is to leverage the unique appeal of your virtual models. Showcase their distinct personalities and lifestyles through engaging content that resonates with your target audience. Whether it's a fashion-forward AI model flaunting the latest trends or a tech-savvy virtual influencer sharing cutting-edge gadgets, presenting them in a relatable light will draw followers in. Use storytelling to create a connection, allowing your audience to feel as if they know these models personally.

Consistency is key in the world of social media, and this holds true for AI-generated models as well. Establish a regular posting schedule that keeps your audience engaged and eagerly anticipating your content. Aim for a mix of high-quality images, captivating videos, and interactive stories that highlight your models' lifestyles and adventures. Consistency not only helps maintain interest but also builds credibility within your niche. Utilizing analytics tools can help determine the best times to post, ensuring your content reaches the maximum number of potential followers.

Engagement is crucial when it comes to growing your follower count. Actively interact with your audience by responding to comments, asking questions, and encouraging user-generated content. Consider hosting live Q&A sessions or virtual events where followers can interact with your AI models in real-time. This level of engagement fosters a sense of community, making followers feel valued and more likely to spread the word about your models. Additionally, collaborating with other influencers or brands can expose your AI models to new audiences, further amplifying your reach.

Utilizing hashtags effectively can significantly enhance your visibility on Instagram. Research popular and niche-specific hashtags relevant to your content and incorporate them into your posts. This will help in reaching users who are actively searching for the type of content you offer. Don't hesitate to create a unique hashtag for your AI models that followers can use to share their experiences or opinions. This not only promotes engagement but also makes it easier to track conversations surrounding your models, allowing you to adapt your strategies based on audience feedback.

Finally, consider incorporating contests or giveaways into your strategy. Offering enticing prizes that align with your brand can attract new followers while engaging your existing audience. Encourage participants to follow your account, like your posts, and tag friends to enter. This not only boosts your follower count but also increases overall engagement, as participants are excited to share their experiences with others. By creatively combining these strategies, you can cultivate a thriving community around your AI-generated models, paving the way for a profitable venture on social media.

Utilizing Hashtags and Trends

Utilizing hashtags and trends effectively can catapult your AI-generated models into the limelight on platforms like Instagram. Hashtags are the lifeblood of discoverability, connecting your content with users who are actively searching for specific topics. When you use relevant and trending hashtags, you're not just tagging your content; you're inviting a wider audience to engage with your posts. The key is to research and select hashtags that resonate with your niche while also capturing the zeitgeist of current trends. This tactic can significantly boost your visibility, leading to increased followers and, ultimately, more monetization opportunities.

Trends on social media can change in the blink of an eye, making it essential to stay ahead of the curve. Monitoring trending topics, challenges, and popular content types allows you to align your AI models with what captures the public's imagination. For instance, if a specific dance challenge is trending, consider creating an AI model that participates in it. Not only does this make your content feel timely and relevant, but it also enhances the likelihood of virality. Embracing these trends can help you tap into existing conversations, making your models feel more relatable and engaging to your audience.

Engagement is another critical aspect of leveraging hashtags and trends. The more your AI-generated models engage with current trends, the more people will want to interact with them. Use stories, reels, and posts to create a narrative around your models that resonates with ongoing discussions. Ask questions, encourage user-generated content, and foster a community where followers feel involved. This level of interaction not only builds loyalty but also drives your content higher in the algorithm, making your models more visible to potential followers and partners.

Strategically timing your posts can amplify the effectiveness of your hashtag use. Pay attention to when your target audience is most active on Instagram and schedule your content accordingly. This ensures that your posts have the best chance of being seen and engaged with. Additionally, consider joining forces with influencers within your niche who are adept at using hashtags and trends. Their established audience can help propel your AI models into new circles, increasing your reach and credibility in the industry.

Finally, don't shy away from experimenting with different hashtag combinations and trend participation. What works for one post may not yield the same results for another, so be prepared to iterate based on performance. Analyze engagement metrics to see which hashtags and trends drive the most traffic and interaction. By continually refining your approach, you will discover the most lucrative strategies to monetize your AI-generated models. The world of Instagram is ever-evolving, and those who adapt quickly will thrive in this exciting digital landscape.

Engaging with Your Audience Effectively

Engaging with your audience effectively is the cornerstone of building a successful brand using AI-generated models on platforms like Instagram. The power of social media lies in its ability to connect individuals through shared interests and experiences. When you harness AI models that look and act like real influencers, you have a unique opportunity to captivate your audience with visually stunning content that resonates. By understanding your audience's preferences and interests, you can tailor your messaging to create a deeper connection, ensuring your brand stands out in a crowded marketplace.

To truly engage your audience, start by creating a consistent brand voice that reflects the personality of your AI models. Whether your AI-generated model is fun and quirky or sophisticated and elegant, maintaining a consistent tone across all your posts will help establish a recognizable identity. Use storytelling techniques to share the journey of your AI models, making them relatable and authentic. This approach not only draws in followers but also encourages them to interact with your content, as they feel a genuine connection to the persona you've created.

Visual appeal is paramount in the world of Instagram, and AI models offer limitless possibilities for creativity. Invest time in crafting visually striking posts that showcase your models in various settings and styles, making sure to align with current trends. Experiment with different formats such as reels, stories, and carousel posts. Each format presents a unique opportunity to engage your audience differently. Encourage your followers to participate by asking questions, running polls, or inviting them to share their favorite looks or styles inspired by your AI models. This interactive approach keeps your audience invested and eager to see what you'll post next.

Regularly analyzing engagement metrics is essential for refining your approach. Utilize Instagram's analytics tools to track which content resonates most with your audience. Pay attention to likes, comments, shares, and saves to identify trends in user behavior. This data-driven strategy allows you to pivot your content strategy in real-time, ensuring that you are meeting your audience's needs and preferences. Don't hesitate to experiment with your content based on these insights, as flexibility can lead to discovering new, engaging ways to present your AI-generated models.

Lastly, foster a sense of community around your brand. Engage with your audience by responding to comments, sharing user-generated content, and collaborating with other creators. Create a space where followers feel valued and part of your journey. Hosting giveaways, challenges, or live Q&A sessions can further enhance this sense of belonging. By nurturing these connections, you not only build loyalty but also encourage organic growth through word-of-mouth as your followers share their positive experiences with your AI models. In this vibrant landscape of social media, effective engagement is not just about visibility; it's about creating lasting relationships that drive success.

Chapter 6: Monetizing Your AI Model

Identifying Revenue Streams

Identifying revenue streams is a crucial step in maximizing your profits from AI-generated models on social media platforms like Instagram. With the rise of virtual influencers, there's an exciting opportunity to tap into multiple income sources. Understanding these revenue streams will empower you to strategize effectively and unleash the full potential of your virtual models. Whether you're a seasoned entrepreneur or just starting, there's a wealth of possibilities waiting for you!

One of the most lucrative avenues is brand partnerships. Companies are eager to collaborate with AI models that can attract attention and engage audiences. By positioning your virtual influencer as a trendsetter, you can secure sponsorships that pay handsomely for promotional posts. Brands are increasingly investing in unique and eye-catching content, and your AI-generated model is perfect for that. Create compelling narratives around your model's lifestyle, interests, and aesthetics to make brands want to jump on board!

Affiliate marketing is another fantastic revenue stream. With your AI model promoting products that resonate with its audience, you can earn commissions on sales generated through your unique links. This approach allows for flexibility in partnerships, as you can choose products that align with your model's persona. The more you engage your followers with authentic recommendations, the greater your chances of generating income. Remember, authenticity is key;

audiences can tell when a promotion feels forced, so choose products that fit seamlessly into your model's narrative.

Selling digital products or merchandise is also an exciting option. With the rise of e-commerce, you can create and market exclusive items that reflect your AI model's brand. Think apparel, digital art, or even virtual experiences. By leveraging your model's popularity, you can build a loyal fanbase eager to support and purchase products. Engaging followers through polls and feedback can help you tailor offerings to their preferences, ensuring your merchandise resonates with your audience.

Lastly, consider offering services such as coaching or consultations based on your expertise in creating and managing AI models. As the landscape of virtual influencers grows, many will seek guidance on how to navigate this new frontier. Your knowledge can become a revenue stream by providing valuable insights to aspiring creators. Hosting webinars, workshops, or one-on-one sessions can expand your reach and establish you as a thought leader in the AI-driven social media space. With the right strategy, identifying and developing these revenue streams can lead to an exhilarating journey toward financial success with your AI-generated models!

Collaborating with Brands

In the ever-evolving landscape of social media, collaborating with brands has become a golden opportunity for those utilizing AI-generated models. These digital personas are not just visually captivating; they represent a revolution in marketing strategies. By leveraging the unique appeal of AI models, brands are eager to engage with influencers who can seamlessly integrate these virtual figures into their campaigns. This creates a win-win scenario where brands can reach new audiences and you, as a creator, can monetize your innovative approach to influencer marketing.

When approaching brand collaborations, it's essential to showcase the distinct advantages that AI-generated models offer. Unlike traditional influencers, these virtual models can be tailored to fit any brand's image, aesthetic, or target demographic. They are reliable, consistently on-brand, and can be available around the clock. Highlight how partnering with AI models allows brands to experiment with new concepts without the limitations that come with human models. This flexibility can lead to creative campaigns that resonate strongly with their audiences, showcasing your ability to think outside the box.

Building relationships with brands requires strategic outreach and a professional online presence. Create a portfolio that highlights your previous collaborations, campaigns, and the engagement metrics that demonstrate the effectiveness of your AI-generated models. Brands want to see proof of concept; therefore, presenting clear data on how your models have driven engagement, conversions, or brand awareness will set you apart. Use social media platforms to showcase your work, engaging with brands directly through comments or direct messages, and positioning yourself as an expert in the niche of AI models.

Networking is another critical component in securing brand collaborations. Attend industry events, webinars, and online forums where brand representatives and marketers gather. Engage in conversations about the future of marketing and the role of AI in shaping brand narratives. Your enthusiasm and passion for AI-generated models will resonate with like-minded individuals, opening doors to potential collaborations. Remember, the more connections you make, the more opportunities will arise, leading to lucrative partnerships that can amplify your reach and influence.

Lastly, always maintain a collaborative mindset. When working with brands, be open to feedback and willing to adapt your ideas to align with their vision. A successful partnership is built on mutual respect and understanding, ensuring that both parties benefit from the collaboration. By fostering positive relationships and demonstrating your commitment to delivering exceptional results, you'll not only enhance your reputation in the industry but also pave the way for future collaborations. Embrace the journey, and watch as your AI-generated models transform not just your career, but the entire landscape of influencer marketing.

Selling Merchandise and Digital Products

Selling merchandise and digital products is an exhilarating avenue for generating income, especially when leveraging AI-generated models. Imagine a world where your virtual models not only captivate audiences but also become ambassadors for your brand! These lifelike avatars can showcase a wide range of products, from trendy apparel to exclusive digital content, making them perfect for maximizing profits on social media platforms like Instagram. By tapping into the power of AI, you can create a unique selling proposition that stands out in a crowded marketplace.

The beauty of utilizing AI models lies in their versatility. You can curate a collection of merchandise that resonates with your audience's interests, whether it be fashion, beauty products, or tech gadgets. For example, if your virtual model embodies a chic fashionista, you can collaborate with clothing brands to promote stylish outfits. Each post featuring your AI model could highlight a different product, driving traffic to your online store and enticing followers to make purchases. The key is to maintain a consistent aesthetic that aligns with your model's persona, creating a seamless shopping experience for your audience.

Digital products offer another exciting opportunity for monetization. From exclusive behind-the-scenes content to personalized virtual experiences, the possibilities are endless. You could sell e-books, online courses, or even virtual meet-and-greets with your AI models. By offering unique and engaging digital experiences, you not only generate income but also foster a deeper connection with your audience. Imagine fans excitedly purchasing a digital art piece created in collaboration with your AI model, or enrolling in a course where they learn to leverage AI in their own businesses!

Marketing your merchandise and digital products is crucial for success. Utilize social media strategies that resonate with your audience, such as eye-catching visuals and engaging storytelling. Incorporate polls, giveaways, and interactive content to build excitement and encourage purchases. Collaborating with other influencers or brands can also amplify your reach. By cross-promoting your AI models and their associated products, you can tap into new audiences and expand your customer base.

The potential for profit in selling merchandise and digital products with AI-generated models is immense. This innovative approach allows you to create an engaging online presence while reaping the financial rewards of your creativity. As more consumers embrace the digital landscape, the demand for unique, personalized experiences continues to grow. By positioning your virtual models at the forefront of this trend, you are not just selling products; you are building a brand that resonates with the future of commerce. Embrace the excitement of this journey, and watch as your profits soar!

Chapter 7: Navigating Legal and Ethical Considerations

Understanding Copyright and Ownership

Understanding copyright and ownership is crucial for anyone looking to profit from AI-generated models. As these digital personas begin to dominate social media platforms, especially Instagram, it's essential to grasp the legal landscape surrounding them. Copyright laws are designed to protect original works, including visual content, and understanding these laws will help you navigate potential pitfalls in your entrepreneurial journey. You want to ensure that your innovative creations don't inadvertently infringe on someone else's rights while maximizing your profit potential.

When you create an AI-generated model, you're essentially generating a unique piece of intellectual property. This means that, in many cases, you hold the copyright to the images and content produced by your model. However, the ownership can become complex if you utilize pre-existing assets or datasets to train your AI. It's vital to distinguish what is your original input versus what is derived from protected works. This distinction will not only protect your interests but also enhance the value of your brand in the eyes of potential collaborators and investors.

Licensing agreements play a significant role in the AI-generated model landscape. If you plan to use AI models for commercial purposes, understanding how to properly license your creations is paramount. This includes knowing whether to pursue exclusive or non-exclusive licenses and the terms that accompany them. Awareness of licensing can open up various revenue streams, allowing you to monetize your models effectively while remaining compliant with copyright laws. It's about leveraging your creativity while ensuring you're on the right side of the legal framework.

Moreover, the rapid evolution of technology continues to challenge traditional notions of copyright. As AI models become more sophisticated, questions arise about authorship and ownership. If an AI creates a stunning image that goes viral, who owns that content? Currently, copyright laws may not clearly define this scenario, but being proactive in understanding these emerging issues can position you as a leader in a groundbreaking field. Engaging with legal professionals who specialize in intellectual property can give you a competitive edge and help you navigate these uncharted waters.

Finally, developing a robust strategy for managing your AI-generated content is essential. This includes regularly monitoring how your models are used across social media and being vigilant about potential infringements. Building a strong brand presence will not only attract followers but also create opportunities for collaborations and sponsorships. By effectively understanding copyright and ownership, you will be better equipped to protect your assets while thriving in the exciting world of AI-generated models on platforms like Instagram. Embrace the adventure and let your creativity soar!

Ethical Marketing Practices

Ethical marketing practices are more important than ever in the realm of AI-generated models. As the digital landscape evolves, the lines between reality and virtuality blur, and consumers become more discerning. It's essential for businesses to engage in marketing strategies that are not only effective but also uphold the highest ethical standards. By prioritizing transparency, authenticity, and respect for consumer rights, brands can foster trust and build lasting relationships with their audiences. This approach not only enhances brand loyalty but also positions companies as responsible players in the ever-expanding world of AI.

One of the cornerstones of ethical marketing is transparency. When using AI-generated models, it is vital to disclose that these figures are not real people. This clarity helps manage consumer expectations and prevents feelings of deception. By openly communicating that the models are computer-generated, brands can maintain credibility and integrity. This transparency not only aligns with ethical standards but also empowers consumers to make informed choices. As a result, when followers engage with AI models, they do so with an understanding of the technology behind them, leading to more genuine interactions.

Authenticity is another key aspect of ethical marketing practices. While AI models can be designed to mimic real-life personalities and lifestyles, it is crucial to ensure that the content they represent aligns with the values and beliefs of the brand. Developing a distinct voice and personality for your AI model that resonates with your target audience can create a meaningful connection. Authenticity encourages engagement and fosters a sense of community among followers. By showcasing real emotions and experiences, even within the context of a virtual persona, brands can cultivate a loyal following that appreciates the genuine effort behind the creation.

Respecting consumer rights is paramount in the ethical marketing landscape. This means understanding and adhering to privacy regulations, obtaining necessary permissions for data use, and being mindful of the potential impacts of your marketing strategies. With AI-generated models, there is a responsibility to ensure that the content shared does not promote harmful stereotypes or exploit vulnerable groups. By crafting campaigns that are inclusive and considerate, brands can position themselves as advocates for positive change. This ethical approach not only enhances brand reputation but also attracts like-minded consumers who value social responsibility.

In conclusion, embracing ethical marketing practices when leveraging AI-generated models is not just a moral obligation; it is a strategic advantage. By prioritizing transparency, authenticity, and respect for consumers, brands can create a positive impact in the digital space. As the market continues to evolve, those who commit to ethical standards will not only stand out but will also pave the way for a future where AI and humanity coexist harmoniously. Let's champion these practices to ensure that as we profit from AI-generated models, we do so responsibly and sustainably, ultimately enriching the brand experience for consumers around the globe.

Managing Public Perception

Managing public perception is crucial when venturing into the realm of AI-generated models, particularly in the vibrant world of social media. The first step to building a positive image is transparency. Audiences are becoming increasingly aware of the digital landscape and the technology behind it. By clearly communicating that the models they are engaging with are AI-generated, you establish an honest relationship with your followers. This transparency not only enhances credibility but also invites curiosity, encouraging users to explore the innovative technology behind these captivating figures.

Creating a compelling narrative around your AI models is essential for capturing the audience's imagination. Instead of simply presenting them as digital creations, craft stories that resonate emotionally. Highlight their unique personalities, interests, and lifestyles as if they were real influencers. This approach transforms your models into relatable figures, making it easier for followers to connect with them. Engaging storytelling can facilitate a sense of community, encouraging followers to share their experiences and interact more deeply with the content you produce.

Social proof plays a pivotal role in managing public perception. Showcase the success and popularity of your AI models through collaborations, partnerships, and testimonials. Feature interactions with real users or other influencers, and demonstrate the impact these virtual beings have on social media. Showcasing positive engagement metrics, such as likes, comments, and shares, reinforces the idea that the models are not just computer-generated images but legitimate players in the influencer space. This validation can significantly enhance public perception and inspire confidence among potential followers and clients.

Incorporating user-generated content is another fantastic way to bolster your models' public perception. Encourage your audience to create and share content featuring your AI models. This not only fosters a sense of involvement but also amplifies your reach through organic sharing. Highlighting fan-generated posts creates a community vibe and establishes your brand as approachable and interactive. When followers see their contributions recognized, they become more invested in the models, leading to a more engaged and loyal audience.

Finally, actively manage your online presence and respond to feedback in real-time. Monitoring comments, messages, and mentions allows you to gauge public sentiment and address any concerns promptly. Engaging directly with your audience shows that you value their opinions and fosters a sense of community. By managing public perception proactively, you can cultivate a positive image for your AI-generated models, positioning them as innovative and relatable figures in the bustling world of social media influencers. This strategy not only drives engagement but also opens the door to monetization opportunities, paving the way for success in this exciting niche.

Chapter 8: Scaling Your AI Model Business

Expanding to Multiple Platforms

Expanding to multiple platforms is a thrilling opportunity for anyone looking to maximize the reach and profitability of AI-generated models. While Instagram is undoubtedly a powerhouse for visual content, the landscape of social media is rich with possibilities just waiting to be explored. By strategically positioning your AI models across various platforms, you not only enhance their visibility but also tap into diverse audiences eager to engage with innovative content. This expansion can lead to exponential growth in your brand's recognition and revenue.

Each platform presents unique features that can showcase your AI-generated models in captivating ways. For instance, TikTok thrives on short, engaging videos, allowing your models to participate in trending challenges or create their own viral content. This dynamic format can attract younger audiences and encourage interaction in real-time. Meanwhile, platforms like Pinterest can serve as a visual portfolio, where users can discover and save your models, driving traffic back to your main offerings. The key is to tailor your content to fit the tone and style of each platform, ensuring your AI models resonate with their respective audiences.

Moreover, branching out to platforms such as Facebook, Twitter, and YouTube can open additional revenue streams through advertising, partnerships, and sponsored content. By sharing insights, behind-the-scenes looks, and tutorials featuring your AI models, you can cultivate a community of followers who are not only interested in your models but are also eager to learn and engage. This builds loyalty and trust, crucial elements for sustained success in the competitive world of social media.

Engaging with influencers on various platforms can further amplify your reach. Collaborations with popular creators who align with your brand can provide instant visibility to their followers, some of whom may be unfamiliar with AI-generated models. These partnerships can take many forms, from co-created content to shoutouts, and can significantly boost your credibility in the industry. The more your models are seen and discussed, the more opportunities arise for monetization, whether through merchandise, exclusive content, or affiliate marketing.

Lastly, analyzing performance metrics across different platforms will empower you to make informed decisions about your content strategy. Understanding which models resonate best with audiences on each platform allows you to refine your approach, ensuring optimal engagement and profitability. As you expand your presence, embrace the journey with enthusiasm and creativity. The world of AI-generated models is ripe with potential, and by leveraging multiple platforms, you can turn your innovative ideas into a thriving business that captivates and inspires.

Automating Your Processes

Automating your processes is the key to unlocking incredible efficiency and profitability in the world of AI-generated models. Imagine a scenario where you no longer need to manually post content, engage with followers, or analyze performance metrics. Instead, you can harness the power of automation tools to streamline these tasks, allowing you to focus on scaling your business and maximizing your profits. By leveraging automation, you can transform the way you interact with your audience and boost your income without sacrificing quality or creativity.

First and foremost, consider using scheduling tools for your social media posts. Platforms like Buffer and Hootsuite enable you to plan your content in advance, ensuring a consistent online presence. This is particularly important in the fast-paced world of Instagram, where engagement is key. By automating your posting schedule, you can maintain a steady flow of content that showcases your AI-generated models, keeps your audience engaged, and attracts new followers—all while freeing up your time for other crucial business tasks.

Engagement is another area ripe for automation. Tools such as ManyChat can help you create automated chatbots that interact with your followers in real time. These bots can answer frequently asked questions, provide information about your AI models, and even guide users through the purchasing process. By implementing such technology, you can enhance customer service, create a personalized experience for your audience, and convert casual viewers into loyal customers—all without the need for constant manual interaction.

Analytics and performance tracking should also be automated for maximum impact. Platforms like Google Analytics and Instagram Insights provide valuable data on how your AI-generated content is performing. By setting up automated reports, you can receive regular updates on engagement rates, follower growth, and revenue generated from your models. This allows you to make data-driven decisions quickly, optimizing your strategies and campaigns to ensure you're always on the path to success.

Finally, integrating payment and order fulfillment processes can significantly enhance your business operations. Solutions like Shopify and PayPal offer automated payment processing that can handle transactions seamlessly, allowing you to focus on creating and promoting your AI models. By streamlining these processes, you can ensure a hassle-free experience for your customers and maximize your revenue potential. Embracing automation in these key areas will not only save you time but will also position your business for exponential growth in the exciting landscape of AI-generated models on social media.

Building a Team for Growth

Building a team for growth is an exhilarating journey that can transform your venture into a thriving enterprise. As you embark on your mission to profit from AI-generated models, assembling a talented and motivated team is crucial. These individuals will not only help bring your vision to life but also amplify your reach and impact within the dynamic world of social media. The right mix of creative minds, technical experts, and marketing strategists can propel your project to heights you may never have imagined.

To start, look for individuals who share your passion for innovation and creativity. Seek out talent that understands the nuances of social media platforms like Instagram. Graphic designers, content creators, and copywriters who can craft compelling narratives around your AI models will be invaluable. Their skills will help you create captivating posts that resonate with your audience. When everyone on the team is aligned with your mission and brings unique skills to the table, the potential for growth becomes limitless.

Next, don't underestimate the importance of tech-savvy individuals. Your team should include AI specialists and data analysts who can fine-tune your models, ensuring they perform at their best. They will play a vital role in understanding audience engagement and optimizing your approach. By leveraging their expertise, you can create more realistic and appealing AI models that attract followers and drive engagement. This technical backbone is essential for scaling your operations as you grow.

Collaboration is key to fostering a productive team environment. Encourage open communication and brainstorming sessions where every voice is heard. This not only sparks creativity but also builds camaraderie among team members. When everyone feels valued and part of the process, they are more likely to contribute their best ideas and efforts. A culture of collaboration will lead to innovative strategies that can set you apart from competitors in the crowded social media landscape.

Finally, be sure to invest in training and development for your team. The world of AI and social media is ever-evolving, and keeping your team updated with the latest trends and technologies is crucial. By providing opportunities for learning and growth, you not only enhance their skills but also show that you are committed to their personal and professional development. A well-equipped team is not just a group of employees; they become your partners in success, united in the mission to harness the power of AI-generated models and make a mark on the social media scene.

Chapter 9: Future Trends in AI Modeling

Innovations on the Horizon

The world of AI-generated models is on the brink of a revolution, and the innovations on the horizon are bound to shake up the social media landscape, particularly on platforms like Instagram. Imagine a future where virtual models not only showcase products but also engage with audiences in real-time, providing personalized shopping experiences that feel incredibly authentic. This is not just a dream; it's an imminent reality. Companies are investing heavily in developing AI technologies that enhance interactivity, making these models more relatable and appealing than ever before.

One of the most exciting innovations is the integration of augmented reality (AR) with AI-generated models. Picture this: users can try on clothes or accessories virtually before making a purchase, all thanks to models that can seamlessly integrate into their own environments. This technology is poised to transform the shopping experience, allowing consumers to visualize how products will look on them without ever stepping foot in a store. The potential for monetization is enormous, as brands can leverage these capabilities to drive sales while providing an engaging and interactive experience for their audience.

Furthermore, advancements in deepfake and motion capture technology are making it possible for virtual models to exhibit realistic emotions and expressions. This means that AI models won't just be static images; they will act, dance, and even interact with followers through live streams or video content. Imagine a virtual influencer who can respond to comments and engage with fans in a way that feels genuine and spontaneous. This level of interactivity enhances brand loyalty and creates a community around these AI-generated personas, opening up new avenues for monetization through sponsorships and merchandise.

As AI continues to evolve, we can expect to see a surge in collaborative efforts between brands and virtual models, leading to innovative marketing strategies. Picture a campaign where multiple AI models team up for a fashion line launch, each with a unique personality and style. This creates a dynamic narrative that captivates audiences and encourages them to follow and engage with these models. Brands can tap into diverse markets, utilizing the different personas of these virtual models to reach a wider demographic and generate significant revenue.

Finally, the ethical implications of AI-generated models will also guide the innovations we see in the future. As consumers become more aware of the authenticity of influencers, brands will need to be transparent about their use of AI-generated content. This will lead to the development of standards and regulations in the industry that promote responsible use of technology while maintaining consumer trust. Embracing these innovations not only offers a pathway to profit but also positions businesses at the forefront of a rapidly evolving digital landscape, ensuring that they remain relevant and competitive in the marketplace.

The Role of AI in Influencer Marketing

The emergence of artificial intelligence has revolutionized the influencer marketing landscape, paving the way for a new breed of social media stars: AI-generated models. These stunningly realistic digital personas are capable of captivating audiences just like their human counterparts, but they come with unique advantages that make them an appealing choice for brands seeking to enhance their marketing strategies. With AI models, businesses can create tailored content that resonates with their target audience while maintaining complete control over their brand image. This innovative approach not only boosts engagement but can also lead to increased revenue as companies tap into the vast potential of AI-generated influencers.

One of the most exciting aspects of using AI models in influencer marketing is the ability to generate content at an unprecedented scale. Traditional influencers may have busy schedules and limited availability, but AI models are always on call, ready to create fresh, eye-catching content whenever needed. This flexibility allows brands to maintain a consistent online presence, posting high-quality images and videos that keep their audience engaged. By leveraging AI-generated models, marketers can easily experiment with different styles, themes, and messages, analyzing real-time data to understand what resonates best with their followers.

Another significant advantage of AI in influencer marketing is the cost-effectiveness it provides. Hiring top-tier human influencers can be prohibitively expensive, especially for smaller brands or startups. In contrast, AI-generated models eliminate the need for costly photoshoots, travel expenses, and agent fees while still delivering professional-quality content. This democratization of influencer marketing means that even businesses with limited budgets can create impactful campaigns that drive engagement and conversions, leveling the playing field in the competitive world of social media.

Moreover, AI models offer brands the opportunity to craft a distinct narrative that aligns perfectly with their values and goals. Unlike human influencers, whose opinions and personalities can sometimes diverge from a brand's vision, AI-generated personalities are designed to embody the exact image a company wants to project. This alignment ensures that every piece of content is on-brand and resonates with the intended audience, maximizing the effectiveness of marketing campaigns. By harnessing the power of AI, brands can tell their stories in innovative ways that captivate consumers and build lasting connections.

Finally, the integration of AI in influencer marketing opens the door to endless possibilities for personalization. With advanced algorithms, brands can analyze user data to create highly targeted campaigns that appeal to specific demographics. AI models can be programmed to adopt various styles, tones, and themes, making it easy to connect with diverse audience segments. This tailored approach not only enhances user experience but also drives conversions, as consumers are more likely to engage with content that speaks directly to their interests and preferences. In this dynamic landscape, the role of AI in influencer marketing is not just a trend; it is the future of how brands connect with their audiences and achieve remarkable success.

Preparing for the Next Wave of Technology

As we stand on the brink of a technological revolution, the potential to profit from AI-generated models has never been more thrilling. These virtual models are not just figments of imagination; they are meticulously crafted avatars that can engage audiences on social media platforms like Instagram, creating endless opportunities for monetization. To prepare for this next wave, it's essential to understand the unique characteristics of AI models and how they can be leveraged to captivate followers, drive brand engagement, and ultimately, generate income.

The first step in preparing for the future is to familiarize yourself with the tools and technologies that power AI-generated models. From advanced algorithms to cutting-edge graphic design software, the landscape is constantly evolving. By investing time in learning about these tools, you position yourself at the forefront of this burgeoning market. Explore platforms that allow you to create or customize virtual models, understanding how their features can be harnessed to create compelling content that resonates with your audience. The more adept you become at using these technologies, the more opportunities you'll have to innovate and stand out in the crowded social media space.

Next, consider the diverse niches available for monetizing AI models. Whether it's fashion, fitness, beauty, or lifestyle, each niche offers unique ways to engage with followers and brands. Identify your target audience and tailor your virtual models to appeal to their interests. Create captivating stories and scenarios that showcase your models in relatable contexts, making them feel authentic and desirable. By strategically positioning your AI models within specific niches, you can attract sponsorships and collaborations with brands looking to tap into your engaged audience, leading to lucrative opportunities.

Building a strong online presence is crucial in this digital age. Utilize platforms like Instagram not just to showcase your AI models but to create a brand around them. Share behind-the-scenes content, engage with followers through polls and Q&As, and leverage trending hashtags to increase visibility. The more interactive and dynamic your content, the more likely you are to cultivate a loyal following. By establishing a compelling narrative around your AI models, you can create an emotional connection that encourages followers to invest in your brand, whether through purchases or partnerships.

Lastly, stay ahead of the curve by continually adapting to new trends and technologies. The social media landscape is ever-changing, and being flexible is key to long-term success. Keep an eye on emerging platforms, evolving user preferences, and advancements in AI technology. Attend workshops, webinars, and industry conferences to network with other innovators and learn about the latest strategies for monetization. By embracing change and maintaining a forward-thinking mindset, you'll be well-equipped to ride the next wave of technology and maximize your profits from AI-generated models. The future is bright, and the possibilities are limitless!

Chapter 10: Real-Life Success Stories

Case Studies of Successful AI Models

In the rapidly evolving landscape of social media, AI-generated models have emerged as revolutionary assets for brands and marketers. Case studies showcasing successful AI models illustrate the immense potential of this technology to generate revenue and enhance engagement. Companies are harnessing the power of AI to create hyper-realistic digital personas that resonate with audiences, driving traffic and sales like never before. By analyzing these successful implementations, aspiring entrepreneurs can glean valuable insights into how to leverage AI-generated models for their own profit.

One standout example is the virtual influencer Lil Miquela, who has captivated millions on Instagram. Created by the tech company Brud, Lil Miquela is not just a digital avatar; she has her own personality, style, and narrative that she shares with her followers. Brands such as Calvin Klein and Prada have partnered with her, tapping into her vast audience to promote their products. This collaboration demonstrates how AI models can seamlessly integrate into marketing strategies, offering a fresh and modern approach to influencer marketing that drives engagement and sales.

Another compelling case is the rise of Shudu, the world's first digital supermodel. Created by photographer Cameron-James Wilson, Shudu has graced the covers of Vogue and collaborated with luxury fashion brands. Her lifelike representation and striking visuals have redefined beauty standards in the fashion industry. By utilizing Shudu, brands can engage with a diverse audience while avoiding the complexities and costs associated with traditional modeling. The success of Shudu highlights the potential for AI models to not only generate revenue but also challenge industry norms, creating new opportunities for brands to connect with consumers.

The fashion brand Balenciaga has also embraced the AI model phenomenon. By incorporating virtual models in their marketing campaigns, Balenciaga has successfully blended creativity with technology. These AI-generated models showcase the brand's cutting-edge designs in ways that traditional models may not achieve, allowing for unique storytelling and artistic expression. The results have been astounding: increased brand visibility, engagement, and sales. This case study exemplifies how brands can innovate and remain relevant in a digital-first world through the strategic use of AI models.

Lastly, the case of the AI-generated model Noonoouri is worth noting. This virtual influencer has gained a loyal following by advocating for sustainability and ethical fashion. Noonoouri collaborates with brands that align with her values, effectively driving awareness around important social issues while promoting products. Her success illustrates how AI models can be more than mere marketing tools; they can serve as powerful voices in the social conversation, attracting consumers who prioritize ethics and sustainability in their purchasing decisions. By learning from these case studies, entrepreneurs can harness the potential of AI-generated models to create unique and profitable ventures in the world of social media.

Lessons Learned from the Pioneers

The journey into the world of AI-generated models is paved with the insights and experiences of pioneers who first ventured into this exciting terrain. These innovators have not only harnessed the power of artificial intelligence but have also shared valuable lessons that can propel newcomers toward success. Their stories highlight the importance of creativity, adaptability, and a willingness to experiment in order to capitalize on the lucrative opportunities that AI models present. Embracing these lessons can lay the groundwork for aspiring entrepreneurs to make their mark in the rapidly evolving landscape of social media.

One key lesson from the pioneers is the significance of understanding the target audience. Just as traditional models cater to specific demographics, AI-generated models must also resonate with their followers. The pioneers emphasized the need for thorough market research to identify trends and preferences within different niches. By analyzing what engages audiences, new entrepreneurs can create AI models that not only attract attention but also foster a loyal following. This targeted approach can lead to higher engagement rates, translating into increased monetization opportunities through brand partnerships and sponsored content.

Another essential takeaway is the power of storytelling. Pioneers in the field have demonstrated that successful AI models do more than just look good; they tell a story that captivates and connects with their audience. Crafting compelling narratives around these virtual models can enhance their appeal, making them more relatable and engaging. By integrating elements of authenticity and personality, aspiring entrepreneurs can transform their AI models into influencers that resonate with followers, ultimately driving higher engagement and revenue.

The importance of continuous learning and adaptation cannot be overstated. The pioneers of AI-generated models have shown that the digital landscape is ever-changing, with new technologies and trends emerging at a rapid pace. Staying ahead of the curve requires a commitment to ongoing education and experimentation. Embracing new tools and techniques, as well as being open to feedback from the audience, can lead to innovative strategies that keep AI models fresh and relevant. This adaptability not only enhances the models' performance but also solidifies their position in a competitive market.

Lastly, collaboration is a theme that resonates strongly among the pioneers. Many of them have found success by partnering with other creators, brands, and influencers to amplify their reach and impact. These collaborations can take various forms, from cross-promotions to joint campaigns that leverage each party's strengths. By fostering a spirit of cooperation, aspiring entrepreneurs can tap into new audiences and resources, creating a synergistic effect that propels their AI model endeavors to new heights. The lessons learned from these trailblazers serve as a powerful reminder that success in the world of AI-generated models is not just about individual brilliance but also about building a supportive network that fosters growth and innovation.

How You Can Follow in Their Footsteps

In the ever-evolving landscape of social media, the emergence of AI-generated models presents an exhilarating opportunity for aspiring entrepreneurs. If you're eager to tap into the lucrative world of virtual modeling, following in the footsteps of successful pioneers is not only inspiring but also strategically beneficial. These trailblazers have harnessed the power of AI technology to create captivating personas that attract significant attention and, ultimately, revenue. By studying their methods and adapting their strategies, you can carve your own niche in the realm of AI-generated models and start your journey toward financial success.

To begin, immerse yourself in the art of content creation. Successful AI models thrive on engaging and visually stunning content that resonates with audiences. Explore various themes, styles, and aesthetics that capture the essence of your virtual persona. Utilize AI tools to enhance your visuals, ensuring that each post is not only eye-catching but also authentic to your brand. Remember, consistency is key; develop a posting schedule that keeps your audience eagerly anticipating your next update. By crafting a compelling narrative around your AI model, you can foster a loyal follower base that is excited to engage with your content.

Next, leverage social media platforms to maximize your reach. Instagram, with its visual-centric approach, is the perfect playground for AI-generated models. Engage with your audience through stories, polls, and live sessions, creating an interactive experience that deepens their connection to your virtual persona. Collaborate with influencers and other creators within the niche to expand your visibility. These partnerships can introduce your model to new followers and potential clients, amplifying your growth trajectory. Don't shy away from experimenting with different types of content, such as reels or IGTV videos, to see what resonates most with your audience.

Building a strong brand identity is another crucial step in following the success of established AI models. Your AI-generated persona should have a distinct personality, style, and voice that sets it apart from others in the market. This uniqueness will not only attract followers but also create opportunities for monetization. Consider ways to diversify your income streams, such as sponsored posts, brand collaborations, or merchandise. By aligning with brands that reflect your model's identity, you can create authentic partnerships that resonate with your audience and generate revenue.

Finally, stay informed about the latest trends and advancements in AI technology. The digital landscape is continually changing, and keeping up with these shifts can provide you with a competitive edge. Attend workshops, webinars, and conferences focused on AI and social media marketing to expand your knowledge and network with like-minded individuals. By continuously learning and adapting, you can refine your strategies and optimize your approach to creating and monetizing your AI-generated model. Embrace the journey, and remember that the path to success is a combination of creativity, strategy, and perseverance.

www.ingramcontent.com/pod-product-compliance
Lightning Source LLC
Chambersburg PA
CBHW070427240526
45472CB00020B/1573